BRADF
MEMO

Part of the
MEMORIES *series*

Contents

First published in Great Britain by True North Books Limited, England HX3 6SN. 01422 244555
www.truenorthbooks.com |
Printed and Bound by Short Run Press Ltd, Exeter.
Text, design and origination by True North Books
Part of the 'Memories' compact series and based on the original Bradford Memories publication.

A busy Market Street in the mid 1940s.

Introduction

Welcome to Bradford Memories, a look back on some of the places, events and people in the city which have shaped the lives of local people of around half a century. The following pages are brought to life by a selection of images from the not-too-distant past, chosen according to their ability to rekindle memories of days gone by and show how people used to shop, work and play in the area where they grew up. It is hoped that the following pages will prompt readers own memories of Bradford from days gone by - and we are always delighted to hear from people who can add to the information contained in the captions so that we can enhance future editions of the book.

There is a growing appetite for all things 'nostalgic' and we are pleased to have played a small part in swelling the number of images and associated information available to the growing number of enthusiasts. There is much talk in modern times about the regeneration of the local economy, the influx of new industries and the challenge of attracting new enterprise from other regions to Bradford. 'Change' is relentless and the photographs on the page in the book serve to remind us of some of them. So sit back and enjoy the ride, as we take you through a pictorial meander through the streets of our great city.

WILL'S CAPSTAN
SERVICE POOLS
SERVICE POOLS
HALFORD
DRESS YO

Around the city centre

Tram lines still snake through Town Hall Square in a view which is unrecognisable today. As we look along Tyrrel Street towards the Wool Exchange, Thornton Road leads off towards the left; further still to the left once lay the historic New Inn, once a popular Bradford watering hole. Market Street gives a twist past Burtons, with the Town Hall out of sight on the right. What a host of memories come flooding back! Halfords corner, where a sun blind protects the goods on display in the window from fading; Farmer Giles, a pleasant and cosy milk bar where we often stopped off for a glass of milk, a quick cup of tea or coffee and a snack; the splendid Collinson's Cafe, where diners were entertained by a string and piano trio; Burtons gents outfitters, where thousands of Bradfordians were smartly kitted out through the years. All gone now, of course. These buildings in Tyrrel Street and Market Street were doomed; the high-rise National and Provincial Building Society (which was to stand empty by the end of the 20th century) and Centenary Square would one day replace them. At the time of our photograph traffic was light by today's standards, but kept in order all the same by the ever-present police officer on point duty. The area is now, of course, virtually free from traffic except for public transport.

The Forster Square of the 1920s bore little resemblance to the square with which we are familiar at the beginning of the 21st century. The tall buildings to the left of the photograph (bottom right) no longer exist; they stood where Broadway approaches Forster Square today. The map of Victorian Bradford is a fascinating study; it shows us exactly how the city changed through the 20th century. Back then, Broadway simply didn't exist; it was created when the buildings between two narrow streets, Watkins Alley and Ship Alley, were demolished. Forster Square was the terminus for a number of trams, and as only the more affluent Bradfordians owned a car, public transport was the accepted way of getting around the city. The photographer of old has captured a scene bustling with life as people sort themselves into orderly queues to board their trams. The trams were convenient to those travelling to and from Bradford by train - Forster Square Station takes up much of the background in this shot, with the impressive Midland Hotel to its left - fortunately still with us today and very much alive. As we all know, the same cannot be said of the station. Future years would see an L-shaped block of modern buildings built in front of it. A new entrance to the station was created to the rear, where a lift brings passengers wishing to get to Cheapside up to street level. Elevator-haters face a tough climb.

In an interesting shot which the photographer very probably recorded on the same day, we turn and look in the opposite direction, where the Co-op sale is in full swing, and hordes of scurrying shoppers crowd the pavement hoping to spot a bargain (above right). This was probably the time of the annual sales, which of course were always held in January (unlike today, when stores seem to find any excuse to hold a 'sale').

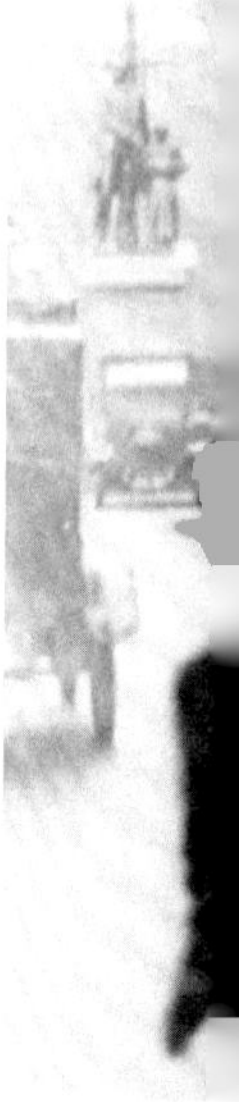

This building housed the Co-op until 1940, when Lingards moved in and stayed until the building was demolished in 1959. Market Street leads off to the right of the photograph. Behind and to the left of the trams, the 19th century reformer William Oastler reaches out to protect the children who slaved for up to 14 hours a day in Yorkshire woollen mills, where overlookers beat them to keep them awake, and many were maimed for life by falling into moving machinery. Oastler agitated for a shorter working day; success came in 1847 with the Ten Hours Act, which limited the hours of work for women and children between 8 and 13 to 58 a week. Oastler's statue now stands in Northgate.

Princes Way, with its heavy load of nose-to-tail traffic, today cuts across this view of the Bradford of yesteryear, on its way towards Godwin Street. The roundabout which once marked the bottom of Manchester Road is merely a memory, and the fine block of buildings which once housed the well-known business of bookmaker Fred Truelove was one of the many victims of the city's redevelopment. 'Zip Goes a Million' was showing at the Alhambra at the time of our photograph. The war memorial, right, has become so much a part of the city's scenery that we pass it without really seeing it. The memorial, designed by city architect Walter Williamson, was made from stone quarried locally at Bolton Woods. A vast crowd of 40,000 watched as it was unveiled on 1st July 1922 - the 6th anniversary of the Battle of the Somme. The memorial was set up to honour the memory of those who gave their lives in the 'war to end all wars', the Great War of 1914-1918, of whom around 5,000 were from the Bradford area - the majority of them our gallant 'Bradford Pals'. The two bronze figures on the memorial depict soldiers advancing with bayonets fixed; the bayonets, which in the wrong hands could have done somebody a real mischief, were later removed.

Dark satanic mills.... It's hard to say just where this evocative image was caught by the camera. One suggestion is that it could have been the Ingleby Road area looking towards the city centre, but who knows? The fact is that it could have been anywhere in the Bradford of our childhood, when black smoke belched from scores of mill chimneys, wrapping every building in a black shroud of soot and peppering the washing on every clothes line. Young readers may think this is a scene from Dante's Inferno, yet it is all too real to those of us who remember the resulting 'pea soupers' - those thick yellow fogs that turned day into night and made it impossible to see more than a yard or two ahead. A nightmare for drivers, creeping at a snail's pace behind the faint red rear lights of the driver in front. Thousands of coal fires around the city added their smoke to the fog, creating what came to be known as smog - a deadly mixture of smoke and fog that caused countless traffic accidents, and brought on bronchial problems. We do not have the figures for Bradford, but in London in 1952 the deaths of over 4,000 people were directly linked to smog. It was all to change with the passing of the Clean Air Act in 1955.

A mini-roundabout today marks the spot where the photographer stood to capture this view of Fair Road in Wibsey. To the right, little except the names above the shops and businesses has changed. The traffic is something else; take a good look at the road in those long-ago days when it had only one vehicle - and that one was parked at the kerbside! The row of low shops on the left offered a variety of goods and services. There was the National Provincial Bank, Hudson's Chemist's shop, a draper's, a tobacconist's - handy for a bag of sweets or a packet of Woodbines to take into the cinema - and right at the end, a branch of the well-known Bradford gents' outfitter O S Wain. These single-storey shops stood in front of the Cosy Cinema, whose entrance, slightly higher than the shops, can be seen towards the end of the row. All gone now, and replaced around 1980 by the modern Co-op supermarket. The Cosy was a firm favourite with local cinemagoers. Opened on 4th June 1930 - Whit Monday - the Cosy (advertising 'Super Talkies at their Best') had a total of 761 seats. Were you there to see 'Doctor in Love'? The cinema's last film before it closed for ever in March 1961.

Natural curiosity makes us wonder where all these ladies are going as they head off, all in the same direction, down Holroyd Hill in Wibsey. Though the buildings may have been modernised and the picturesque old gas lamps replaced, the scene is nevertheless instantly recognisable. Today, of course, we must add a stream of fast-moving traffic to what was then - we would guess in the 1920s - a quiet road in a tight-knit community. Could these pedestrians have stepped into the future they would be able to shop for groceries at Alldays on the left beyond the trees, browse in the second hand shop, eat at the Balti House further down, or pick up a Chinese takeaway on the way back at the shop on the right. The take away food they were used to, however, did not run to the exotic - a fish and a penn'orth was good enough for them! As respectable ladies, of course, they would not have been expected to darken the doors of the Holroyd House Hotel on the left.... The building facing up Holroyd Hill once housed the Co-op where these ladies perhaps did their weekly shopping; it still exists, with its date clearly visible - 1898.

Hey's Ale was once on offer at the Rawson Hotel, whose lovely architecture, together with that of Rawson Market, has been little appreciated over the years. At the time of our photograph, the market frontage is bricked up, awaiting the extensive redevelopments in the late 1950s. Air raids were a rarity in Bradford during World War II, but Rawson Market was one of the few casualties. The adjoining fish market came to the rescue, offering places for stalls that had occupied the ruined western end of the market; it was 1958 before the first phase of the reconstruction was completed. When the market reopened it was every housewife's choice. Beef, pork and lamb; apples, pears and bananas; cabbage, sprouts and carrots - they were all there, and much more besides. One stall went in for the less well known and more exotic, such as aubergines, broccoli and mangoes - produce we see in everyday use today. A cheese stall and a delicatessen added variety. All gone, of course, along with the building itself, by the end of the 20th century. Many stallholders moved on to a temporary market in Westgate - unfortunately well away from the main shopping area - where they still await the building of yet another construction on the site of the old Rawson Market.

HOTEL
LES
RAWSON HOTEL

A Number 9 trolley bus heads up Leeds Road for Thornbury, and a string of heavily loaded lorries turn into Well Street. This view from the rooftop of the Junction public house was about to change; an exoskeleton of scaffolding already surrounds a block of warehouses, ready for demolition. The 1960s ushered in a time of drastic change and upheaval in the city. But 20/20 hindsight began to make its mark, and in 1973 Little Germany (the buildings to the right in our 1960s photograph), a development built between Church Bank and Leeds Road, was declared a conservation area. Magnificent buildings such as Law Russell House, built in 1874, and the Chinese Export warehouse in Vicar Lane (1871) were constructed by German Jewish textile merchants who had made their home in Bradford during the 19th century. Fortunate to survive the 'clean sweep' when much of the city centre was lost for ever, the area we know today as Little Germany became part of Bradford's 'tourist trail'. Vicar Lane, originally the pathway used by the vicar on his way to and from the parish church - crosses the main Leeds Road from left to right in this shot. The parish church of St Peter in nearby Church Bank became Bradford Cathedral as recently as 1919.

A few stoical pedestrians brave muddy shoes as they use the walkway provided by the construction workers across a site on which, until a short time earlier, blocks of buildings had stood. Piles of stone flags, rubble and a generator still mark the spot. Modern shops and offices have now been constructed here, so this open view of Britannia House is no longer possible. The Gas Showroom still had their premises in Britannia House at the time, as did the offices of the Cunard Line. However, the store that is best remembered in the corner position is that of the gents outfitter, O S Wain. Osborne Sayer Wain - perhaps better known to Bradfordians as 'Ossie' Wain - must have been a remarkable man; he was certainly one who was not afraid to take a risk. Britannia House, after all, was well away from the rest of the city centre stores, where the vast majority of go-ahead businessmen wanted to set up shop. Ossie Wain, however, was not deterred; he took on what was in effect a white elephant and turned it into one of the best-known tailors in Bradford. His son took up the reins when he died in 1962; O S Wain's closed down in 1987.

HARDY & CO
BURTON
GERRARDS

As conspicuous as the nose on Pinnochio's face, the new 'square box' constructions rise alongside the old city centre buildings. Alongside the National Provincial Bank on the right, Boots towers skywards. Many of us had forgotten that Boots once had a large store here - its rear door was between the bank and Wilson's. Remember Wilson's? And the pleasant and friendly cafe above the popular clothing store, where shoppers could rest their weary feet and eat a reasonably priced meal in comfort? Over the thirty or so years that have passed since their construction, these buildings have acquired a certain nostalgia of their own. On the other side of Broadway, British Home Stores is not yet ready for opening, and the hoardings are still up. Young's jewellers, Burtons, Hardy's and other businesses, however, are already up and running in the new building. How strange it seems now to see traffic passing along Broadway, which has been a pedestrian only area for many years. This spot, seen from the Midland Hotel, was to see the extending of Cheapside and the building of Petergate on the far side of the new buildings. The two main thoroughfares would meet at a large roundabout in Forster Square.

By the early 1950s it was becoming obvious that conditions in many areas of Bradford were woefully inadequate. Long terraces of back-to-back houses or single storey cottages were commonplace, and bathrooms, for many, were an undreamed-of luxury. Washing and shaving took place in a small scullery - and a call of nature, whatever the weather, meant a trip down the yard, along the street, or across the road. Toilets, which were often shared by two or more

families, were often grouped together in unattractive yards in the centre of the terrace of houses. Yes - the era of the 'guzunda' had still not ended. And for younger readers who may not have heard the term before, the piece of equipment in question was so called because it 'guzunda' the bed.... We draw a veil over the personal necessities of the day, but young mothers must have longed with all their souls for somewhere better to bring up their families. It was time, the council decided, to act, and 'compulsory purchase' notices were sent out by the hundred. Many couples, however, were horrified when they realised that the purchase price being offered for their homes fell far below the amount they would need to buy another property. In some places - Clayton, for example - prefabs presented a temporary solution, and the people who were used to doing without bathrooms and using outside toilets fell in love with the surprisingly spacious little bungalows, which had bathrooms, separate toilets, built-in cupboards and modern kitchens. Council houses offered other families an improved lifestyle, and as the crowded old terraces disappeared in the city's 'slum' clearance scheme, smart new estates such as this one in Thorpe Edge - built where open fields had been a short while before - began to spring up around the city (top). In many areas, the only way was up, and following the modern trend in housing, tower blocks began to reach for the sky (left). It was only much later that the nowfamiliar problems began to arise, which turned a few large estates into ghettos and some tower blocks into 'no go' areas. By the 1990s the problems were being addressed, and recent years have seen the demolition of many of the highrise flats and the introduction of regeneration schemes which have marvellously transformed many of our rundown estates.

The Picton Street Flats still smelled of fresh paint when the brand new blocks were pictured from the air back in 1957 (below). Our airy viewpoint gives us the advantage of taking in the innovative design of the new flats, which themselves were quite an innovation back in the 1950s. They were built as a result of the clearance and redevelopment scheme in the Green Lane area, off Lumb Lane. The new residents, who were more used to living in a close knit community of terraced houses, had mixed feelings about living in flats. After all, you can build a house, but a home must grow, and some were reluctant to let go of a whole way of life. How would they get along with new neighbours? Would there be a lot of noise from families above, below, and to either side? Others, however, were eager to seize the new opportunity to enjoy modern facilities - an up to date kitchen; a bathroom with hot water on tap - and blessedly, an indoor toilet! The school, seen here bottom right, was convenient for the children - all they had to do was cross Green Lane, which cuts across the photograph from left to right. Green Lane joins Lumb Lane at the right edge of the view; Southfield Square runs along the length of the far side of the flats, which still stand today. In many places, tower blocks like filing cabinets for people have not proved to be successful, and at the beginning of the 21st century some have already been demolished. As early as the 1920s and 30s, overcrowded houses had become a problem across the city, and when the second world war ended the Council's new housing schemes really swung into action. Thorpe Edge saw the building of hundreds of houses that were 'fit for heroes', and our pigeon's eye view over Rockwell Lane and Northwood Crescent shows off the smart new estate at its best (above). Not all local people welcomed the building of the large council estate, however, as it was built on an area of open land. St John's Church was eventually built on the empty site to the right. One private car and a van sum up the traffic level at the time, though as post war prosperity really kicked in, a family car became a reality to most people, and future years would see a great deal more traffic in Thorpe Edge.

Events and occasions

Hordes of enthusiastic Bradfordians gather outside the Norman Arch, spreading across Manningham Lane and into the park, to give a right royal welcome to their distinguished visitor. This scene is a typical example of the way Bradford has greeted members of the royal family, and over the years we have welcomed many different Royals to our city. Our immediate problem is identifying the occupants of the leading, open-topped car! Unfortunately, we can only speculate. Prince Philip visited Bradford back in January 1949 to officially open the new Bradford Grammar School, a stone's throw away from Lister Park; he was on his own that day as Princess Elizabeth, as she was then, had only recently given birth to Prince Charles. He was back again in October 1954, and this time the Queen was with him; a memorable occasion, this, to the 20,000 Bradford schoolchildren who gathered in Park Avenue cricket ground to greet the royal couple. A view of the top of their heads as they drove past was all that could be seen by those unlucky enough to have taller people standing in front of them - which includes this author! But the children could still sing (with more gusto than talent), and the Queen and the Duke were suitably treated to a rendition of the many verses of 'On Ilkla Moor Baht 'At'.

Drawn by the drama of the moment, a knot of bystanders cluster around the site of what could have been a very nasty road accident. Perhaps the West Yorkshire bus, standing across the road, had also been involved, and these people had been passengers on the bus? Unfortunately we will probably never know what caused this Model 'T' Ford to overturn, or find out whether its driver escaped the incident without injury. Traffic accidents had become a problem by the 1930s Between the end of the first world war and 1930 - a mere 12 years - the number of cars on Britain's roads increased from around 200,000 to more than a million, and between the two world wars a staggering total of 120,000 people were killed in traffic accidents.

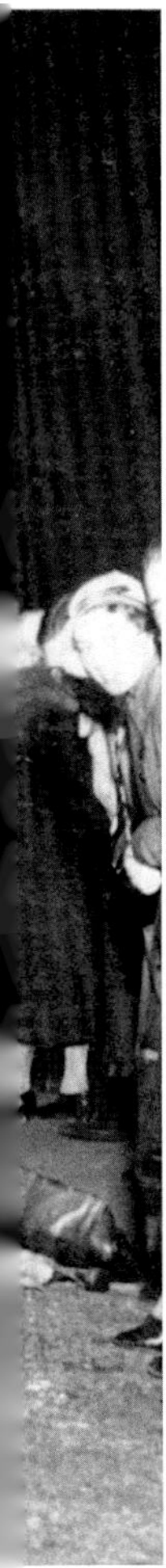

Above: Trying the shining helmets for size, perching atop the extending ladders, swarming all over the vehicles, and no doubt deafening everyone with the bells, these young people are having a whale of a time at one of the open days held at Bradford's fire station. One of 'the most modern and up to date fire stations in the United Kingdom' was how Bradford's Lord Mayor, Mr W C Lupton, described the station at its opening ceremony on 28th October 1902. This was an grand opening in every sense of the word, marked by displays from the brigade and followed by a Town Hall lunch with the Lord Mayor. Built in Nelson Street at a cost of £16,000, this amazing building really was a facility to be proud of. Extensive stables for the horses which drew the fire engines of the day were an important part of the new building, while the 84ft long engine house itself had six bays. A 100-yard drill hall was built at the rear, while the up-to-the-minute facilities for the crews included a billiards table and a gym. Sixty years on, the same spot in Nelson Street saw the building of Bradford's next new fire station, opened in October 1969.

An ultra-modern kitchen was every housewife's dream as long ago as the 1930s, and when Busbys staged a home appliance demonstration every seat was taken. Which of these ladies' hearts did not beat faster at the thought of owning a brand new gas cooker, the latest thing in instant hot water boilers, or the newest gadget to make washing day that little bit easier? A lot of fur is in evidence in the room, indicating that a good number of these ladies had a bob or two tucked away. But for many, it was all an impossible dream, and they would leave the realms of cloud-cuckoo land and return home, roll up their sleeves, and light the fire under the old set pot. Knowing people's circumstances, however, Busbys offered further inducement: if you couldn't buy it, why not hire it? The poster on the wall lists the rental charges for these desirable appliances - a new cooker, for example, would set you back between 3/6d and 9/- a quarter. A real bargain - though the cooker, of course, would never be yours to keep. How many of these housewives, we wonder, signed the agreement before they went home? We know now, of course, that war would break out in 1939; it would soon be time to tighten their belts, make do and mend, and dream on.

Part of Westgate is roped off and scaffolding poles lie ready for use as Corporation workmen clear up after the city's worst night of wartime bombing. August 1940 had seen two earlier raids, the first of which was centred around Heaton Woods and the second saw minor damage from just four bombs. The heaviest raid began on the last night of the month. People took cover and listened fearfully as a total of 116 bombs fell in and around the city; it must have seemed never ending to those sitting in cellars, below the stairs, and in air raid shelters, wondering whether they would be the next victims. Lingard's department store took the full force of a bomb which destroyed the building, with its unusual cone-shaped towers, and set the store ablaze from end to end. The adjoining British Shoe Company and a chapel around the corner in Kirkgate were also extensively damaged. Thirtytwo stalls at the western end of Rawson Market, and seven street-facing shops, were destroyed, and the New Vic cinema (later the Gaumont, then the Odeon) all suffered damage in the same raid. Lingards would later set up shop across the road, and the store on the corner of Westgate and Godwin Street became a familiar Bradford landmark.

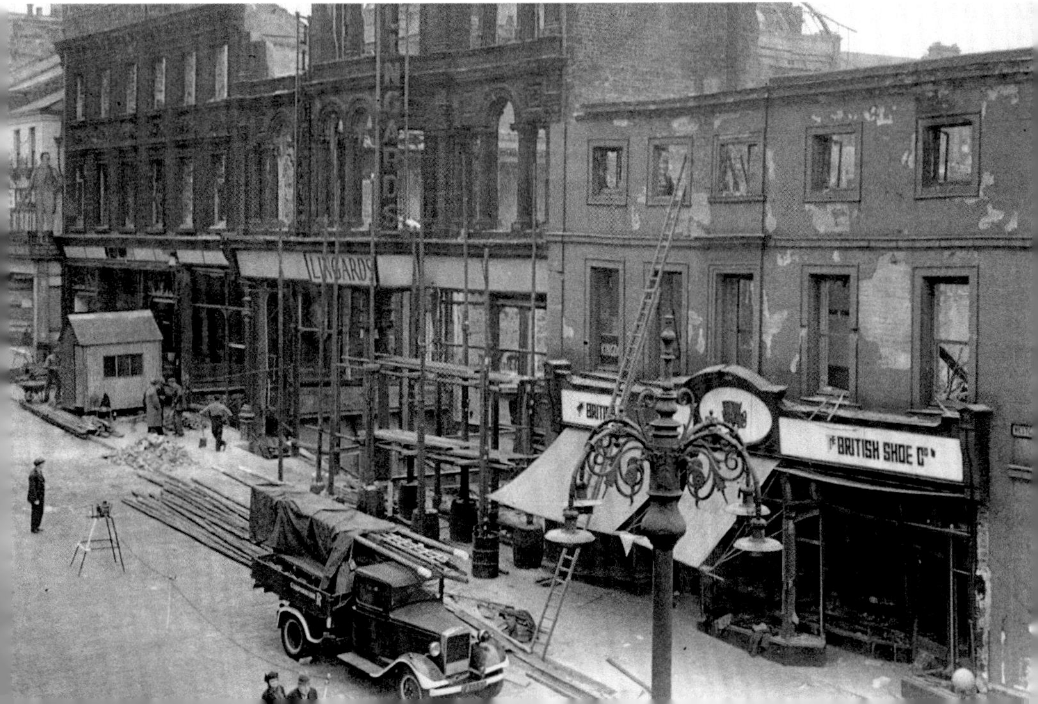

These three WVS ladies and driver are pictured here standing by their vehicle, in their not so attractive gas masks, ready for whatever Nazi Germanymight throw at us. Even before war broke out, millions of gas maskshad already been manufactured in Britain. Notices pinned up on every wall reminded people to carry their masks with them: 'Hitler will send no warning - so always carry your gas mask'. The Women's Voluntary Service was one of the best examples of the successful mobilisation of the energies and abilities of women in the service of the Nation and their contribution to the war effort cannot be underestimated.

The year 1953 signalled the beginning of a 'new Elizabethan age' when our Queen was crowned in a Westminster Abbey service on 2nd June - a spirit which was taken up by the designers of this amazing vehicle used in Bradford's Coronation celebrations, whose exquisite replica of Sir Francis Drake's galleon 'Golden Hind' links Elizabeth I with our present Queen. It was an unforgettable sight for those who viewed this model in all its glory, complete with waves of twinkling lights to represent the sea below. The galleon was created at Thornbury works - and the vehicle on which it was mounted started life in 1929 as single deck one man bus Number 380, the only Leyland Lioness owned by Bradford City Transport. In 1937 it was used as a display vehicle for the coronation celebrations held when George VI - our Queen's father - came to the throne, so celebrity status was not new to this fine vehicle!

'God save the Queen!' was the sentiment echoed all across the city back in 1953. Union jacks flapped gaily in the breeze outside Busby's - in fact the management decorated the entire length of the store frontage with union jacks, tasteful banners, colourful flags and red, white and blue garlands. Many people had been reduced to tears when they heard of King George VI's death from lung cancer in February 1952, and he had been genuinely mourned by the whole nation. But his daughter, who had begun her training for the throne early, when Edward VIII's abdication in 1936 made her the heir presumptive to the throne, was already a popular figure, and along with the rest of the nation Bradford took Queen Elizabeth II to their hearts. Those old enough to remember the coronation will remember the fun, the colour, and the excitement of the occasion. This lovely old photograph brings memories flooding back. Shopping at Busbys (who merged voluntarily with Debenhams in 1953) was a real experience. The enormous store was a firm favourite with Bradfordians for many years. This elegant and beautiful building was doomed, however; fire raged through the building in 1979, and the store disappeared from the Bradford map.

At leisure

To many, this well-loved city centre cinema was the ABC. But to older readers - some of whom may even remember its opening in May 1939 - it will for ever remain the Ritz. 'The Citadel', starring Robert Donat and Rosalind Russell, was the 2,037-seat cinema's very first film, with Joseph Seal entertaining the audience at the cinema's powerful three-manual Compton organ. 'Kiss Me Kate' (a film loosely based on Shakespeare's 'Taming of the Shrew') was top of the bill at the time of our 1950s photograph, and the added attraction was '3-D'. Viewed through cardboard glasses with green and red lenses, three-dimensional films were an interesting curiosity which may have temporarily lured the punters away from their TV sets. But the rot had already set in, and the knell of doom had sounded for Bradford's cinemas.

Odsal has been at the forefront of many aspects of rugby league and holds many records relating to the sport and its supporters. Built back in the 1930s, it was in 1951 that Stanley Wardley, the City Engineer, recognised the old stadium's potential for becoming the Wembley of the North. Never inclined to anything on a small scale, Wardley planned sweeping new developments at the ground which would lead to an eventual capacity of 92,000. Originally the dressing rooms were built at the top on the stadium's rim and players had a long trek down hundreds of steps to the playing area.

At half-time during games most of the competing teams went into a huddle on the pitch rather than start back up the steps.

When many people think of Odsal one image springs to mind. The picture of the then world record breaking crowd for a rugby league match. The crowd at Odsal on 5 May, 1954, for the Halifax v Warrington Challenge Cup Final replay was officially announced as 102,569, however it is widely acknowledged that the correct figure should have been in the region of 120,000.

When it was decided the replay of the final was to be at Odsal, nobody realised that the capacity of the stadium would ever be under threat. Played on a Wednesday, the kick-off was changed to 7.00pm to avoid the rush hour traffic. The first game had been a less than sparkling affair, and the fact that Laurel & Hardy were playing at the Alhambra on the same night, the size of the crowd was not expected to be excessive. On the day there were 00 gatemen and 150 policemen on duty, more than enough for the expected crowd of around 70,000. How wrong they were!!

The record attendance for a domestic, non-final Rugby League match was, 69,429 at the third round Challenge Cup tie between Bradford Northern and Huddersfield in 1953.

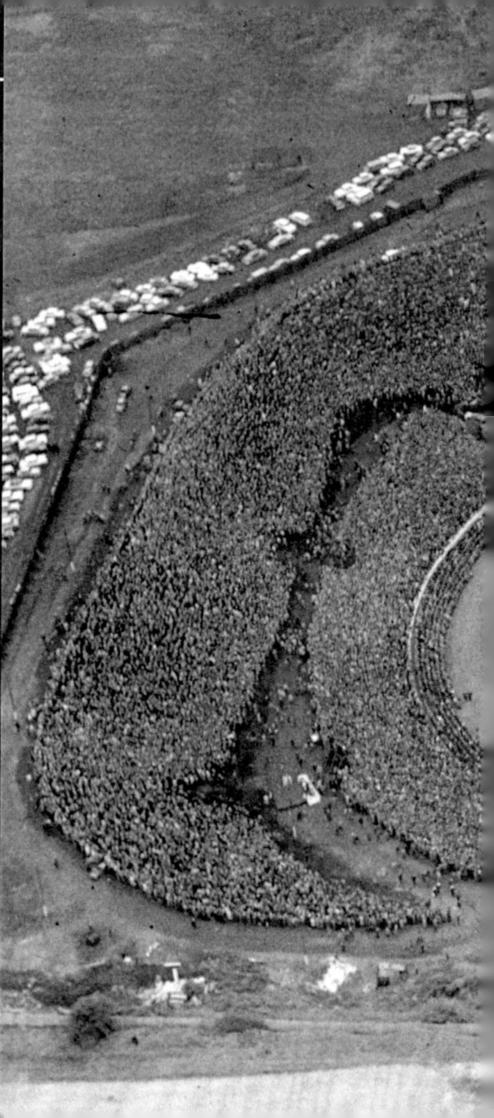

H·A·M·M·O·N·D·S
EXPORT UNITY

Left: Fred Trueman might look more familiar to us with a cricket ball in his hand, but he appears to handle a shovel very competently all the same. His enthusiasm for the task in hand makes us think that at any minute he'll remove his sheepskin jacket, roll up his sleeves, and get down to some real work! But contrary to appearances the great cricketing legend had not been recruited by the construction industry; this was the traditional 'topping-out' ceremony, performed for Bradford in 1963 by 'Fiery Fred' when the foundations for the multi-storey Arndale House were laid. A member of the Yorkshire County Cricket Club - and English Test Match cricketer - Freddy Trueman was one of England's fastest bowlers in his day. With 'Yorkshireman' woven through him like a stick of Blackpool rock, the great man became known across Britain as a real 'character' whose broad accent and uncompromising, 'tough as nails' cricketing skills were a legend. Arndale House, with its many offices, businesses and shops such as the well known Stead & Simpson shoe store, was built on the site of the beautiful and sadly mourned Swan Arcade. The Victorian shopping arcade was built during the 1870s on the site of the White Swan Inn, and was named after the ancient Bradford watering hole. The arcade sang its 'Swan Song' in 1962.

Right: This is an excellent view of the ornate entrance gateway to Cartwright Hall on North Park Road, which has been held to represent "Bradford Baroque", a style of architecture typical of Bradford. The civic art gallery stands in Lister Park, about a mile from the city centre in the Manningham district. It was built on the former site of Manningham Hall using a gift of £40,000 donated by Samuel Lister and it is named after Edmund Cartwright. The opening of the Hall was performed by Lord Masham on 13 April, 1904. It initially had a display of artworks loaned from other galleries and private collections until it was able to purchase a permanent collection of Victorian and Edwardian works. The purpose-built gallery enjoys scenic views of the city and is home to a collection of permanent works, from Old Masters to 20th century British paintings and sculpture. Cartwright Hall also has a biennial open exhibition and contemporary and historical exhibitions by local, national and international artists.

From 'Puss in Boots' to 'The Nutcracker' and from 'Whistle Down the Wind' to 'Cats', the Alhambra has given us enormous pleasure ever since we were old enough to sit on one of the theatre's plush seats and shout 'he's behind you!'. Remember the 'flying ballet'? The Sunbeams? The twelve John Tiller Girls? Marvellous stuff! Francis Laidler is a name that virtually every older Bradfordian will recognise, though few of us know that his background was in brewing rather than in variety. He was 35 when the lure of the stage took him from the brewery and into theatre management. He was the proprietor of the Princes' Theatre in Little Horton Lane when a nearby plot of waste land came up for sale. Laidler bought the land, and his impressive Alhambra theatre, boasting graceful pillars and elegant domes, opened in 1914. The building cost Laidler less than £20,000 - though that was a huge amount of money in the first half of the 20th century. Thankfully the old theatre is still with us - though it was a close thing, demolition having been on the cards back in 1983. A petition was signed by 25,000 protestors, including Sir Lawrence Olivier. EC aid helped to save the day, and tasteful refurbishment transformed the tired old theatre into the jewel in Bradford's crown. Below: Long before the widespread popularity of our 'cheese and onion toasties', Busby's was already offering the delicacy which would one day become a favourite lunchtime snack. And those delicious doubledecker beef-and-salad-filled sandwiches - 'grilled or plain' - cost just 1/2d. If you preferred their 'shilling tea', however, the asking price included a cream tea, a slice of fruit slab cake, and a pot of tea. What a bargain! Younger readers will not remember Busby's, 'The store with the friendly welcome', or their delightful and wellknown logo depicting four marching soldiers. Situated on the fringe of the city on Manningham Lane, Busby's was well away from Bradford's main shopping centre. Even so, from the time Ernest William Busby set up in business in 1908, at first in a small way in Kirkgate, he never failed to show a profit. He moved to his Manningham Lane premises in 1930, where he opened new departments including his famous restaurant and snack bar. During the store's early years, when male office workers wore bowler hats and the ordinary 'man in the street' stuck to his flat cap, diners in Busby's restaurant were often given a personal welcome by Ernest Busby himself, wearing his tall top hat.

For once, Bradford is sunny and warm - and when the sun comes out, so do the swimming costumes! And if you have no bathing cap, who cares? There are few days in the average Yorkshire year that are warm enough to brave the elements, but this day is obviously one of them. Unfortunately we have no date for this delightful photograph, but the style of dress worn by the young mum on the left suggests the immediate post-war period. The Lido - which for those not 'in the know' was Bradford's only outdoor swimming pool - was built in Lister Park in 1930, and was probably the 'Number One' popular local attraction on hot days. Diving boards of varying heights challenged swimmers to attempt daring feats; only the bravest souls dived in from the top board (left). Others with less experience (or less courage?) stuck to entering the water feet first from the side of the pool, with their noses firmly pinched between finger and thumb! Sliding into the water with squeals of enjoyment was a great deal more fun than the serious 'I can dive off the top board' stuff, and on busy days you had to wait your turn for the slide in a queue that went from the ground to the top of the ladder. Sadly, Bradford has many more cold days than hot, and when spending cutbacks threatened the future of the Lido, it was no surprise to hear of the closure of the openair pool in 1973. Even ten years on, however, many were campaigning for the Council to reopen the Lido.It was finally demolished in 1991; a sad but understandable loss to the city.

On the move

On 22nd September 1939 - a fortnight from the outbreak of the second world war - petrol rationing was introduced across Britain. Rationing, based on the horsepower of your vehicle, was to stay in place until 26th May 1950. In addition to the strict rationing, the price of petrol per gallon rose in 1940 to 1/11d a gallon - around double its cost in 1935. For a number of drivers, gas was the answer, and some vehicles, like this Morris Commercial lorry, were converted to run on a fuel which at least was home produced and did not have to be imported from overseas. The Garden Dairy Morris gives us a fascinating glimpse down the years; the bag itself, fully charged with inflammable and explosive gas, looks seriously vulnerable.

A lovely old trolley bus stops in Commercial Street, Shipley, to pick up passengers bound for Saltaire. The value of buses as mobile advertisement hoardings has long been recognised; this one advises sufferers from rheumatism and influenza to use Cephos. ('See what?' went the words of the old TV advert....) This view is vastly different today as many of these buildings - including the Pavilion de Luxe cinema on the left - were demolished when Shipley was redeveloped in the 1970s. Remember those Saturday matinees, when hordes of bubblegum chewing children descended on the cinema? Roy Rogers and his faithful Trigger, the Lone Ranger, Superman, the dog Lassie - they were all there. The whole programme was enlivened by cheers and jeers, flying bits of rubbish, and the shouts of 'Put a penny in!' that harassed the long suffering projectionist when the film broke, as frequently happened. Talkies were still a distant dream when the 630-seat Pavilion de Luxe opened back in 1914. The new cinema boasted an exciting double helping of entertainment, with 'A Question of Right' and 'The Bugle Call' on offer to tempt the punters in. Sadly, it closed in November 1956, to become home to Jarvis bookmakers until the bulldozers moved in in the 1970s.

10
STANNINGLEY
10
JACOB'S
CREAM CRACKERS

In a soot grimed Leeds Road the camera has captured a patient queue (interestingly of men only), who wait to board a Number 10 tram on their way to Stanningley. Was this taken at the end of a working day, we wonder, when those lucky enough to have a job would find a hot meal waiting for them, and after that, perhaps an hour at the Dog and Duck? The bottom of Leeds Road was the terminus for the Stanningley trams, which accounts for the long queue. Bradford hung on to its trams long after most cities had sent theirs to that great tram shed in the sky; services to Odsal and Horsfall Playing Fields continued until as late as 1950. This marvellous photograph was taken in those long ago days which few of us can remember, when the tram was in its heyday. Of the other two forms of transport included in the shot, the old horse and cart was sadly nearing the end of its useful life, while the motor vehicle on the right, typically overtaking both the cart and the tram, was very definitely on the up. Few will recognise the building on the right, but as far as we can make out it stood where Britannia House stands today, dating this view to pre-1926.

How many years is it since our city centre roads were cobbled with those countless thousands of granite setts, the laying of which must have been an enormous task? Bradford has had its trolley buses since the Lord Mayor, proposing 'Success to rail-less trolley traction', set the first one in motion on 20th June 1911. The initial service, however, was limited to the run between Laisterdyke and Dudley Hill, as car Number 240, in its smart livery of prussian blue and ivory, was for a time the city's only trolley bus! By the late 1930s the service was well established, so our photograph is probably pre-war. Amazingly, the Town Hall - now the City Hall, of course - is the only feature pictured here which still exists today. Older readers, who may well have spent many cold, wet and miserable minutes queuing here for the No 37 Clayton trolley, will recognise the view as the end of Thornton Road. Was this photograph taken to mark a particular occasion, we wonder? The driver stands smartly to attention alongside his (untypically) gleaming vehicle, and virtually every passenger waiting in the queue appears to be aware of the photographer.

Thornbury works' yard is the setting for this proud display of Bradford's three forms of public transport. The picture was especially posed back in 1935 for the frontispiece of a new timetable, the three vehicles wearing their Corporation livery of prussian blue and ivory lined out in gold leaf and white; it was 1942 when the light blue and primrose with which we are more familiar was introduced. Two of the three modes of public transport are no longer with us. The draughty old trams were the first to go, though Bradford had its trams far longer than most cities. Bradford was the last trolley bus operator in Britain. As the 1960s dawned, one by one the wonderfully smooth and silent trolleys followed the old trams to the breakers yard as more motor buses began to arrive. Trolley Number 844 was chosen to become Bradford's - and Britain's - very last trolley bus. On Sunday 26th March 1972, crowds gathered outside Duckworth Lane depot as early as four o'clock in the morning to take their farewell journeys on the old trolleys. All that day, every vehicle was filled; the final trolley left for Thornton at 10.57pm with 76 passengers - the maximum load.

CHARLES SIDNEY LIMITED
FOR
39
Charles Sidney Limited
39
FINE CARS
Daimler
LANCHESTER

Left: Readers may have a little trouble placing the premises of Charles Sidney until we remind them that Sidneys' fine car showroom once stood at the junction of Grattan Road and Westgate. Sidney's had a marvellous selection of vehicles on offer: Daimler, Mercedes Benz, Lagonda, Ford and Aston Martin are all advertised in the showroom windows. How fascinating it would be to peep inside and take a closer look! Rimmington's driver appears to have parked his truck outside the doorway of Sidney's (lowering the showroom's tone just a tad), and popped off to do a bit of shopping - though perhaps he fancies driving something a little more stylish, and is browsing among the beauties on show inside! This building was eventually demolished, though the adjoining auctioneers' premises still survives. Further along Grattan Road we can just about glimpse the building which would one day become the city's fascinating Colour Museum. Well worth a visit.

Right: The Post Office clock informs us that it is 5.25, and as shops and offices across the city close at the end of another working day, their employees head for home. The great rush for the buses has begun again - only well-heeled Bradfordians owned their own car during the 1940s, when this view was captured. In the days before the Interchange was even a sparkle in its designer's eye, Forster Square was the terminus for numerous bus routes. These open sided bus shelters provided little protection from the driving rain and malevolent winds of a typical Bradford winter; how many readers have huddled in queues beneath these same shelters as they waited for their trolleys and trams in days gone by? The old Forster Square Post Office, opened in 1867, was in its heyday at the time of the photograph. Wasn't there a scheme at one time to demolish it so that Bradford's magnificent cathedral, tucked away behind it, could be seen and appreciated? The Victorian Post Office building, however, is of real architectural value in its own right, and short of dismantling it stone by stone and rebuilding it elsewhere, the Cathedral is doomed to forever peep at Forster Square over its chimneys!

Readers will perhaps scratch their heads and puzzle over this photograph for a few minutes as they try to pinpoint this spot - which is hardly surprising, as the buildings in this shot except those in the far distance no longer exist. This is Broadway as it was in the 1950s, a date emphasised by the fashions and by the splendid cars which were typical of the day. This was a time when men such as these smart businessmen leaving the 'Gentlemen's Smoking Cafe' on the left still wore hats and 'Inspector Columbo' macs! Ladies' fashions, however, had changed swiftly after the end of the second world war, as full and generous calf length skirts replaced the skimpy 'no fuss' styles of the days of clothing coupons. Car design, too, was undergoing a transformation during those post war years.

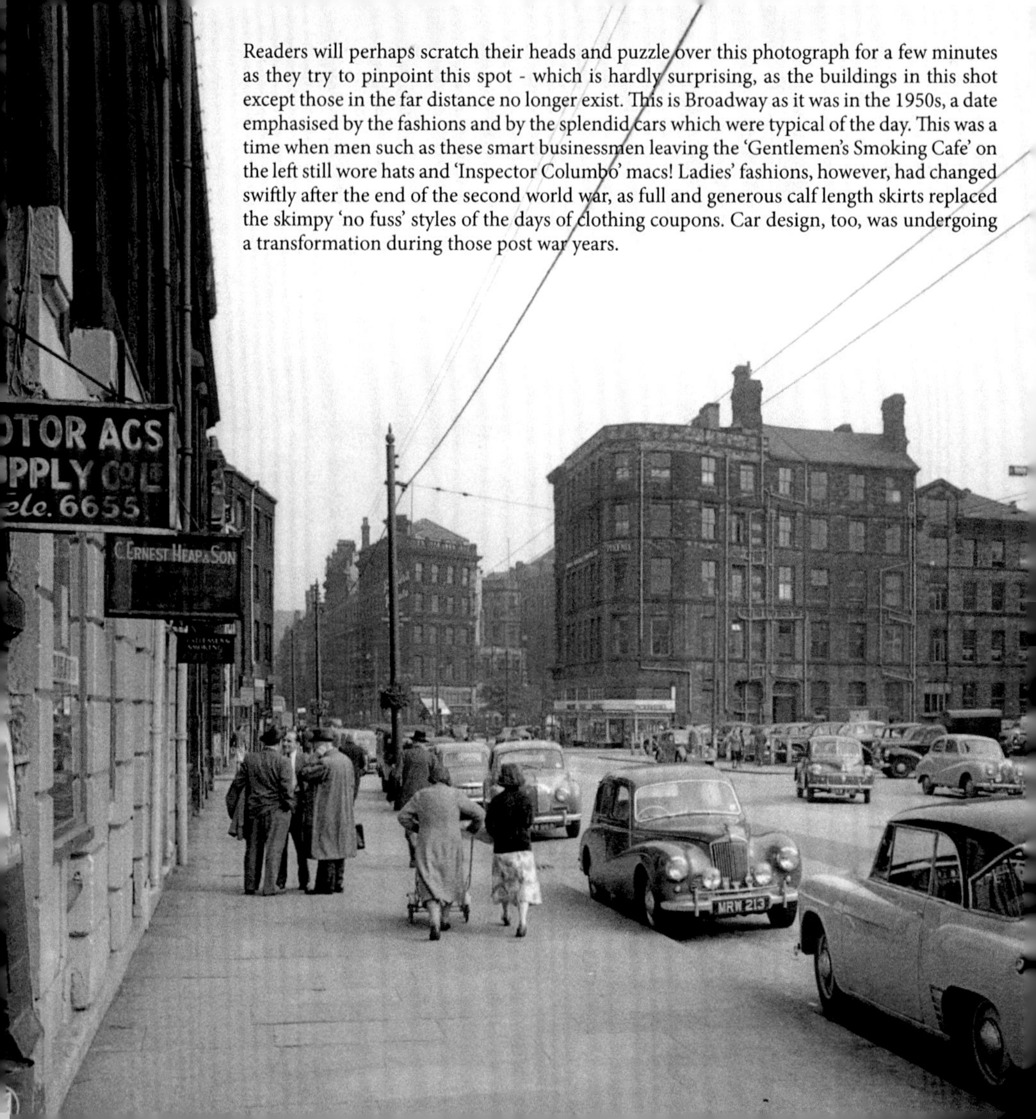

The driver of this sulphuric acid tanker poses proudly at his wheel beside the open gates of Leathers Chemical Company's Northbrook Vitriol Works, which was situated, as far as we can gather, in Canal Road. The company was an old established one, having been founded, amazingly, back in 1750. We cannot say just where Leathers first set up in business, though it could not have been in Canal Road as the Bradford Canal between Shipley and Bradford wasn't built until 1774! Very few businesses can lay claim to a history that goes back to the days when George II was on the throne, when secret Jacobites still drank toasts to Bonnie Prince Charlie, the 'King over the water'! What prompted the taking of this photograph, we wonder? Was it to mark an anniversary or some special event? If so, the tanker itself is a credit to the occasion, as it positively sparkles with polish and 'elbow grease'. Sulphuric acid was, at least at the time of the photograph, commonly used in a great many industrial processes, and it was a well known fact that when the consumption of sulphuric acid increased, it was an indication that industry in general was doing well.

Bird's eye view

Like a Toytown village built from Lego bricks, Bradford's new shopping area, centred around Broadway and Forster Square, lies below us. The circular meeting of the subway system at the junction of Leeds Road, Hall Ings and Petergate, can be easily spotted at the foot of the shot. The domed rooftops of the Exchange Station were still in situ at the time of the photograph; the last train ran from here in 1970, and the station was demolished in 1976. The tall block near Eastbrook Well was Wolfe and Hollanders' furniture store; to its left, Tapp & Toothill's, the well-known stationery store, and behind it, C&A, sadly missed when it closed down in 2001. C&A's rooftop car park was already in use. Petergate, a wide road created by the demolition of old warehouses in Well Street, was still under construction at the time and not yet open to traffic. Though a row of shops and offices was built opposite the new block, Petergate remained a bit of a backwater in spite of the very popular Fine Fare supermarket adjoining Wolfe & Hollanders, and British Home Stores - now popularly abbreviated to BHS. The days of the Ritz/ABC cinema in Broadway were numbered.

Above: Ask any Bradfordian which part of old Bradford he or she was most fond of, and the answer will almost always be Kirkgate Market, with the Swan Arcade coming a close second; the market's ridged rooftops are easily recognised from our lofty viewpoint. A splendid market, Kirkgate had just about everything, from jewellery and second hand books to stylish hats and flowered overalls. Its main entrance was in Kirkgate, which runs from top to bottom on the left of our photograph; remember Hilda Lincoln's flower shop, the first sight to greet you as you mounted the steps and went through the doors? The top entrance was in Godwin Street; spot the rooftop of the old Rawson Market, now no longer with us, though a facade has at least been preserved. Darley Street, running from left to right along the side of Kirkgate Market, has long been - and still is - at the heart of Bradford's busy shopping centre. Today, of course, we have the Arndale Centre, which has established itself in the affections of a new generation of Bradfordians.

The demolition of old properties in Broadway has begun - the thin edge of the wedge - and C&A, British Home Stores, and other modern shops will soon take their place. The Swan Arcade, opposite the Ritz, was still with us at the time; but vast changes were on the cards as building after building was flattened and the city centre we know today began to emerge. Spot the distinctive rooftops of Kirkgate Market on the right, and towards the top of the picture, the twin domes of the Gaumont cinema. Forster Square, bottom right, was still surrounded by tall old buildings when this scene was captured. The old Post Office, on the bottom edge of the shot, still survives, though no longer as a working Post Office. It was replaced by a new modern building near the station, itself now defunct.

Town Hall Square and the Town Hall itself give us a point of reference in the foreground of this early 1960s aerial view. Immediately to the right, Norfolk Street passes between the Town Hall and a block of old warehouses which were later demolished; the pleasant Norfolk Gardens were eventually laid out on this spot. From Town Hall Square Market Street leads up towards the right, past Brown Muff's and the Wool Exchange, ending at Forster Square Station, whose station roofs and goods yard take up the top right corner of the scene. The stately Midland Hotel, on the corner of Cheapside, adjoins the station. Spot the many-ridged rooftop of Kirkgate Market, in the upper half of the photograph.

It has been said that a camel is a horse designed by a committee, and the 'camel' designed by Bradford's planning department was emerging when this scene was recorded around 1969. Take a good look at the empty spaces in the shot and be reminded of the historic core of Victorian Bradford, where so many thriving shops and businesses once stood. Across the road from the library, just left of centre, the Jacob's Well public house was the only old building to survive the new road developments surrounding the roundabout at the junction of Manchester Road and Princes Way. The cleared land to its right stands ready for the construction of the new central police station and magistrates' courts. The foreground of the view is taken up by the extensive site which would become Bradford Interchange, with the multi-storey car park nearby. The empty space adjoining the car park would see the building of the Norfolk Gardens Hotel, later the Stakis. The Town Hall, of course, is easily identified; not too far away, the new Provincial House is already under construction.

Familiar landmarks to the 'old 'uns' - a foreign land to readers born in the 60s and 70s! From the bottom left corner, where Church Bank passes the Cathedral, we move upwards to the stately warehouses of Little Germany; then the long arched rooftops of the Exchange Station, demolished in 1976, can be seen on the left; in the top left corner stands the Victoria Hotel; to its right is the splendid St George's Hall, opened in 1853 (echoing down the years to many a carol service and school Speech Day); the Bridge Street goods warehouses opposite were demolished to make way for the new Interchange. Adjoining St George's in Hall Ings are the offices of the Telegraph & Argus. Sunbridge Road and Kirkgate come in from the top right corner, while to the bottom right is Forster Square Station. In the centre, as subtle as a crimson sparrow, the new C&A building is under construction between Hall Ings and Broadway. On the other side of Broadway, sites have been cleared for new stores which would house Boots' the chemist (later Mothercare), and H Samuel's jewellery store. Nearby is the slightly curved rooftop of the Ritz cinema and directly opposite, between Broadway and Market Street, is the Swan Arcade - both buildings sadly doomed. Across Market Street, spot the triangular-shaped Wool Exchange, once the world's most important woollen market.

This pigeon's eye view of the city centre in the 1930s gives us a peep behind the scenes, revealing just how much we miss when we only view Bradford's buildings from shop window level. Tiny attic windows which open across the rooftops, small courtyards hidden behind the familiar shop fronts, and the elegant Italianate style of the Town Hall's 220ft high clock tower. This was a pleasant sunny day, and, in the centre of the photograph, a whole row of dazzling white sun blinds protect the goods in Brown Muff's windows. Until the mid 1800s few ready made clothes were available; suit and dress lengths were usually bought and made up at home or by tailors and dressmakers. Messrs Brown and Muff, however, recognised a gap in the market when they saw one, and their off-the-peg clothing was a hit with shoppers from the 1850s on. One of our favourite stores, Brown Muff's became House of Fraser in the late 1970s. We can see that construction work of some kind was in progress on the Brown Muff building at the time of the photograph - and interestingly, at the corner of Bank Street and Broadway (on the far right), the site for the Bank Street Post Office has been cleared.

SAXON
GUINNESS
PRUDENTIAL
TOBACCO & CIGARS

Shopping spree

This was Sunbridge Road from Bridge Street, and the block to the right of the shot was looking its age, like a lady approaching the big '6-O' and longing for a makeover. But sadly demolition, rather than restoration, lay only a decade or so ahead from these 1946 views. On the corner of Market Street we can just make out the pillars in front of the shop which at one time was the premises of 'Ann Teek', whose descriptive name says it all, and at the time of the expiry of lease prior to its demolition was Timms & Dyason's glass and china shop. Remember their beautiful panes of curved glass? Across Market street can be seen that rarity in Bradford - a building which survived the wholesale demolition of the heart of the city. Rimmington's, one of Bradford's oldest chemist's shops, still survives here though Butterfields opticians, on the corner of Tyrrel Street, eventually disappeared. Less fortunate was the old but well-used Mechanic's Institute (its upper rooms extended over the Saxone shoe shop on the left of our photographs), whose walls resounded over the years to the varied sounds of concerts and choirs, political speeches and fervent evangelism. The Mechanic's Institute was demolished in 1974.

Next time you walk down Darley Street, raise your eyes above street level and contrast Bradford's Victorian architecture with that of the 1970s, perhaps using the nearby Arndale Centre as a comparison. This fine building with its carved stone pediments above the windows and topped with an ornate balustrade on its corner, is among the precious few which survived the 'clean sweep' of demolition and reconstruction in the mid 20th century. Traffic still travelled up and down Darley Street, Bank Street and Kirkgate, and parked outside its shops, when this scene was captured in the 1950s.

Darley Street buzzes with life in a view which is still instantly recognisable. It's a very long time since we saw traffic in what is now a pedestrianised area; cars approaching from North Parade down the top part of Darley Street are now fed to the right along Godwin Street at this junction. No need for traffic lights here today! Barratts on the left has amazingly survived on this same spot into the 21st century. Few of us, perhaps, will remember the Savoy cinema on the left, as it closed down in 1939. But the Savoy, which opened in 1920, was a large and modern cinema with 1,593 seats. The marvellous old Kirkgate buildings on the right had 52 shops (and the Central Library, which we tend to forget!) facing the busy streets, all built around Kirkgate Market. Constructed at a cost of £83,381, this well loved facility was completed in 1878. This was the place to find a bargain, from bed linen and curtains to sheet music. The haberdashery stall was usually surrounded by ladies shopping for ribbon, bias binding, needles, buttons - in fact anything to do with home dressmaking. A hundred shopping years after Kirkgate Market opened, it had been replaced by the ultra-modern Arndale Centre.

The year was 1947, and as the heavens opened and torrents of water poured into the drains, the narrow culverted Bradford Beck was unable to take the strain. The only way was up, and water literally erupted from the confines of the underground Beck, tearing out hundreds of the wooden blocks which paved the Town Hall Square area and Tyrrel Street. The blocks of course floated away, and most of them ended up in Canal Road. This view along Market Street shows us that as the floodwater boiled from the drainage system, pedestrians clung to the slightly higher ground at the junction with Sunbridge Road in the rather forlorn hope of keeping their feet dry. Workmen had already been called out to begin the clearing up operation.

Antique China

Three ladies ignore the zebra crossing in Thornton Road as they head towards the Clayton trolley stop. Fortunately, there is little traffic about, or they could well have ended up looking at daisies from the wrong end.... Their shopping bags hint that this is a Saturday, as does the number of men in the shot, who, in those days of fuller employment, would otherwise have been at work. Walden's showroom window is receiving attention from passers-by who have perhaps detected a bargain. The large sign above the canopy indicates that Walden's are 'The Bedding Specialists'. Certainly bedding and beds, from bunks to doubles, were on offer in the store, but Walden's was also known for its wide range of furniture. Whether you wanted a dining table and chairs, a three-piece suite, a wardrobe or a sideboard, this city centre store could supply it. All the shops and businesses along this stretch of Thornton Road were nearing the end of their lifetime. Halfords corner, Walden's, Taylor and Parsons kitchenware shop - all were demolished. Stand on the same spot today, and you would be looking at Provincial House, later the Abbey National - an enormous construction that dwarfed all other buildings in its vicinity.

We gaze upon Broadway in the 1960s and view history in the making as the Prince is sadly turned into a frog. Almost 40 years on, the kind of mistakes made in the past are today avoided by a Council who over the last decade or so has established a good record in conservation - and a better taste in architectural style! Traffic would eventually be banned from Broadway, though many of us remember parking our cars on the empty sites where these new buildings were constructed. The shops seen here were all occupied at the time of the photograph apart from British Home Stores on the left. Beyond C&A, Burger King would be opened on the opposite corner of Charles Street; further on still we catch a glimpse of the Ritz cinema's white frontage. The largest store on the right of the scene was undoubtedly Boots, whose premises would in due time be occupied by Mothercare when Boots moved to their new store in the Arndale Centre. Mothercare eventually cut down the size of their store, leaving the Charles Street part to other businesses. The premises on the right corner were at the time occupied by Stones; since then a number of different names have occupied the space above the doorway.

This little trip back through time gives us a clear view of houses and open land in the Bolton Road area as we look along Market Street - a view blocked today by modern buildings. Our viewpoint high above the street allows us to see detail in the Wool Exchange on the left which we would normally overlook. The different colours of stone, for example, that emphasise the pointed arches of the windows; the stone faces of prominent figures such as Richard Cobden and Sir Titus Salt - and those elegant spires. At street level we have long had a choice of small shops in the Wool Exchange. Remember Clayden's, whose display of gorgeous lingerie and nightwear tempted many a passer-by to part with a substantial amount of their hard-earned cash? Possibly not yet in residence at the time of this photograph. The Wool Exchange, opened in 1867, was once the hub of Bradford's wool market, and was known throughout the world.

Making a living

The clock on the wall tells us it's 12.05. Lunchtime in anybody's book, and after a long morning's work the staff canteen is well-filled. If you asked us where this photograph was taken, however, we would have to admit that unfortunately its location is a mystery. Unless, of course, you know better.... These factory workers, most of them women (though there are a few men dotted around the canteen) would have started work early, and a well filled plate of steak and kidney pie and mashed potato would have definitely gone the right way. And perhaps with jam roly-poly and lashings of custard, and a mug of strong hot tea to follow, they could just about face the afternoon's work. There is no price list on the wall, but canteen prices have traditionally been subsidised, and these workers would have had a nutritious and filling meal at a very basic price. Most people have a ready smile for the camera, and even the hardworking kitchen staff at their hatch pose for the photograph. Was this taken to mark a special occasion, we wonder? We will never know.

It is now more than 200 years since a Thornton Road mill installed the city's first steam-driven machinery, nailing down the coffin lid on Bradford's well-established cottage industry of wool combing, spinning and handloom weaving. The next century was a difficult one as wool combing machines, one of which could do the work of a hundred men, steam powered spinning machines and power looms were installed, driving many out of work and reducing families to poverty. Many strikes, riots and wage cuts later, the new factory system was accepted and gradually Bradford became 'Worstedopolis'. By the middle of the 19th century a multitude of mill chimneys were breathing their acrid smoke across Bradford like an army of wheezing dragons. The industry grew strong under such men as Samuel Cunliffe Lister, John Foster and Titus Salt, and Bradford became a thriving and prosperous place. With great pride and confidence in their city, wealthy Victorians celebrated their achievements by erecting buildings which were both impressive and elaborate, building for us the Bradford we came to know in the first half of the 20th century. The wool exchange; the new Town Hall; the Prudential Assurance building on the corner of Tyrrel Street and Sunbridge Road; St George's Hall; the Swan Arcade; Kirkgate Market - and Listers' Manningham Mills, caught on camera here in a dramatic night-time shot (above). Its spectacular 250ft high mill chimney - built with an unbelievable eight thousand tons of stone - became one of Bradford's most familiar landmarks. The majestic mills, arguably the most impressive textile buildings in the north of England, were constructed in the 1880s on the site of Samuel Cunliffe Lister's first mills, which burned down in 1871.

The story goes that when fire broke out in the oldest part of the buildings in February 1871 the fire brigade was alerted. An engine set out towards Manningham - but unfortunately the horses failed to make the hill up Westgate! While more horses were being sent for, the fire blazed merrily on and was soon beyond control. Lister took his heavy losses on the chin and started over. Seven years later, in 1878, the new building was up and running, and Samuel Cunliffe Lister drank a toast in champagne from the top of his magnificent new chimney. He had always striven for excellence, and the quality of Listers' fabrics became known in the highest circles. Samuel Cunliffe Lister died in 1906, but excellence remained the company's trademark; our 1940s photograph (right) shows women burling and mending - that is, carefully checking fabrics for knots and faults.

Workers' playtime, and after a hard day's work at Salts Mills - the largest employer in Shipley - it's clocking off time, and workers eager for a good meal and 'Double Your Money' head for the great outdoors (left). Known in the old days as 't'penny oile', this particular gateway was where workers of old paid a penny fine if they were late for work - and in the days of early starts and no alarm clocks, getting to work on time was a fine art. No 'penny oile' of course in the 1950s when this scene was captured - just black looks for any latecomer from the overlooker! The entire community of Saltaire was founded and supported by just one man, Sir Titus Salt. When the wealthy textile magnate built his Italianate style factory beside the River Aire in Shipley, it was the largest textile mill in Europe and boasted the largest room in Europe Titus Salt - a beneficiary on a grand scale - not only provided work for the people in the surrounding area, but a whole village for them and their families to live in. Saltaire, however, was a dry place for those who enjoyed a pint or three. As a devoutChristian and a strict believer in abstinence, Titus

Salt was very aware of the evils of the 'demon drink', and refused to sanction the building of a public house in his village. The Saltaire mills and village was Salt's final - and most ambitious - project. The much respected benefactor and businessman died in 1876 - but his looms kept going until 1986.

Below: It's 'eyes down' at a factory somewhere in the city - and a stern faced female supervisor in the background is making sure that that's where they stay! Unlike Mike Baldwin's Coronation Street sewing machinists, these girls kept their noses to the grindstone, the gossip to a minimum, and the finished product coming off this labour intensive production line. The days were long, the work often tedious, and when the buzzer sounded at 5.30 the workers were only too glad to switch off their machines and go home. Intensive labour it may have been, but in a city founded on textiles and the huge diversity of processes involved in their production, textiles was where a third of the jobs were - though by the 1930s there was widespread unemployment in the industry. Our photograph dates from the 1940s; we have no way of knowing, however, whether this is a view of much needed wartime production.

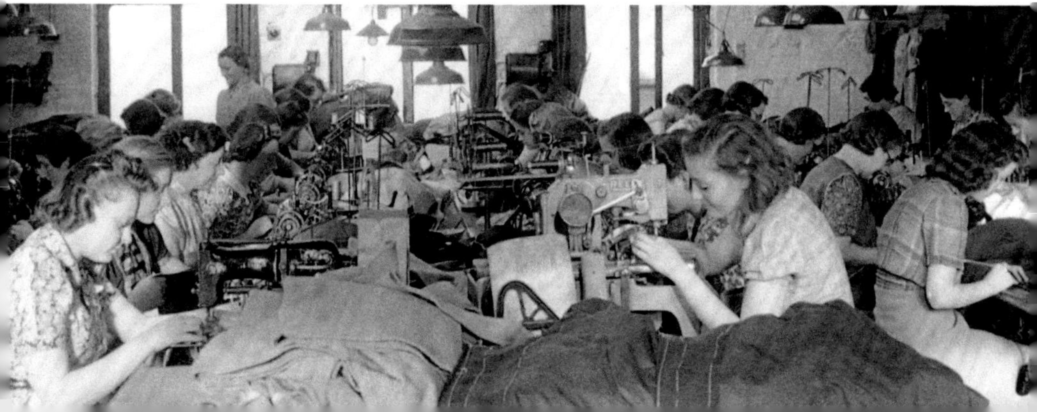

Experiencing a breakdown of your loom was bad enough, but waiting for the overlooker to roll up his sleeves and fix it was about as interesting as watching a plank warp (left). Boredom is etched on the faces of these young weavers; after all, with the overlooker present, they couldn't even make use of the pause in production to enjoy a good chinwag! The girls worked in one of the weaving sheds at Listers' Manningham Mills, possibly (judging by the fashions, and more particularly the hair styles) in the 1930s, when textiles still employed a third of Bradford's workers. The outbreak of the second world war in 1939 took a huge number of men into the services leaving the company operating with a much reduced workforce, yet at the same time propelled Listers' into a flurry of wartime production. The extent of their

involvement was kept carefully under wraps until after 1945, but later figures show that while working for various Government departments during the war, approximately half the company's normal workforce had produced 2,510 miles of parachute fabric, 4,430 miles of silk and nylon parachute cord, and 50 miles of khaki battle dress material, along with thousands of miles of other fabrics including an amazing camouflage cloth which, when coated with rubber, could be inflated to take on the shape of military trucks and tanks - effective dummies to fool the enemy. Though Bradford's textile industry suffered a lot of setbacks after the war, most mills managed to keep going, helped along by the new fabrics such as Terylene and Dacron, which began to take the place of the traditional worsteds.

Our photograph (below), taken sometime during the 1950s, will bring back memories to many of our readers who worked in the industry in years gone by. As the machinery designed during the Industrial Revolution put hundreds of hand workers out of work, so the new technology of the 1960s and 70s brought a similar problem. Smaller companies were unable to invest in the modern methods, spelling the end for the many which went to the wall. The number of textile workers was reduced by half, and the mill chimneys which had for so many years characterised Bradford's skyline gradually began to disappear.

Right: The production lines were buzzing at the Jowett motor manufacturing plant in Idle when this scene was caught on camera. Jowett's built nearly 23,000 vehicles during the 1940s and early 50s. In the foreground, mechanics are working on the popular Jowett Javelin, while a long line of Bradford vans are being built behind. The standard Javelin saloon was well-loved by many, but it was the De Luxe version which, according to Jowett's publicity material of the time, would 'sneak through the air at speed with hardly a ruffle; making 70 seem like 50.' While the standard Javelin sold at £635, the Javelin De Luxe - which could top 80mph - would set you back £735 plus purchase tax. Beautiful as these streamlined cars were, it was the popular Bradford van which really kept the plant bowling along. Whether you were a plumber, ran a laundry or delivered flowers, the Bradford van was the vehicle for you. Its fuel consumption was low, and its two-cylinder, nine-hp engine took it sailing up the steep hills around the city. Though Jowett's sold twice as many Bradfords than Javelins, the firm nevertheless found itself in difficulties in the 1950s. It closed down in 1954 - a sad loss to the city.

Above: Over the years, Bradford has had many different industries apart from its staple, textiles, not least in food production. On the tables are neatly-folded stomachs, on which these men are working; coupled with the mountain of cows' legs piled on a table in the background, we can deduce that the end products of this unidentified factory will be tripe, cow heel, udder and the like. It can't have been the most pleasant job in the world but, as they say, someone had to do it! The tripery, on which we unfortunately have no details at all, was probably linked with the Bradford abattoir in Hammerton Street or perhaps St James's Wholesale Meat Market. How long is it since we saw tripe for sale? Perhaps all those vanished meats which were once commonplace have simply been re-routed into pet foods. Recent food trends have led us to turn up our noses at the kind of meal our grandparents enjoyed. Gone are the days when Granny could call in at the butcher's to pick up some cow heel for Grandad's tea. And we have yet to see the Naked Chef preparing a dish of tripe and onions for his family!

Above: The 1950's brought a return of League derbies with Bradford (PA) following their relegation from Division Two in 1950. In terms of League standing Avenue fared better than City in the first half of the decade although without establishing themselves as serious promotion challengers. In the first derby of the 1950/51 season at Park Avenue on 30 September, City were beaten 1-3 with the official attendance stated as 25,655 (the highest post-war derby crowd).

In the return game of the 1950/51 season in February, 1951 18,454 watched City beat Avenue 4-1. Bradford wore their change shirt for this game which was the same design as that worn by Bradford Northern until fairly recently. Eddie Carr, who scored 56 goals for City in 99 League and Cup games between 1949-53, is seen beating the Avenue keeper to the ball and passing to Whelan (Polly) Ward who scored from close range. Carr and Greenhoff (2) scored the other City goals.

Below: Bradford City players taking glucose as part of their preparation for the FA Cup First Round tie at Derby in November, 1956. The scientific approach obviously had little effect because the Bantams were knocked out of the competition with a 1-2 defeat. John Simm scored City's goal and the attendance for the game was 22,579. Even football 'greats' like Duncan Edwards put their name to glucose tablets. Adverts proclaimed 'Extra Energy Makes the Difference', and were emblazoned with a picture of Edwards in action. This prompted thousands of people to buy the sugar tablets to emulate their idol.

Below: City got off to a great start in 1977/78 with a 4-0 win over Cambridge who had been promoted as Fourth Division Champions. The victory extended the club's sequence of unbeaten home League games to a record 25 dating back to May, 1976. The next win however was not forthcoming until the end of September and City struggled at the bottom of the Third Division all season. After three years in charge, Bobby Kennedy was replaced at the end of January by John Napier. Funds generated from City's successful new lottery were made available for team strengthening. Sadly this could not prevent the club being relegated after only one season in Division Three.

City from left to right: Nicholls, Downsborough, Cooke, Dolan, Wright, Spark, Hutchins, Podd, Watson, Middleton, Fretwell, Hardcastle and Johnson.

Above: In February 1987, Margaret Thatcher wore a Bradford City scarf and was photographed with the team in front of the new main stand at Valley Parade. Following the fire in 1985 the stand was rebuilt and club officials were happy to give the Prime Minister a tour during a visit to Bradford. The 1987/88 season began with City winning the West Riding Cup for the fourth time in succession. During the close season goalkeeper Paul Tomlinson was signed from Sheffield United and defender Lee Sinnott was a £130,000 record signing from Watford. During the first 20 games of the season City won 13 and drew four to stay top of Division Two for ten weeks until the end of November when they were beaten 2-4 at home by Aston Villa.

An aerial view of the city centre taken in the 1930s.

With very special thanks and appreciation for their help and contribution:

Malcolm Burns

Iris Harvey

Brian and Dorothy Burrows

Thanks are also due to Peggy Burns who penned the editorial text and Steve Ainsworth for his copywriting skills